Vine to Wine

Photographed and Written by
Richards Lyon

The author has had expert guidance from John Kongsgaard,
Marco Capelli, Dean Donaldson, William Jaeger, Robert Lamborn,
Ed Weber, and Andre Tschelistcheff............THANK YOU

Copyright © 1999 by Richards Lyon

Second Edition

Stonecrest Press
600 Stonecrest, Napa, CA 94558
(707) 255-8702

Library of Congress Catalog Card Number: 99-70766

ISBN 0-9616004-8-9

Printed in Korea

This photo-essay is the unforseen result of my attempt to understand the basic steps in the creation of fine wine. My camera forays into the vineyards, including ours of 300 plants, opened my eyes to "what is there". I needed to know more. Friends among growers and winemakers patiently and lovingly answered my ever-growing set of questions. Books were read and re-read, their differing points of view adding to the mix, as I sought to discover a simple and direct order (sequence?) that I could understand and retain. My experiences as a member of the small family winery team made me comfortable amid tanks and pumps of the large commercial winery. What I found is here - hopefully to be enjoyed as a learning experience by others like myself, and without claim to expertise.

A wine begins as a branch of a grapevine specially chosen for its ability to withstand serious diseases that limit its growth or destroy it. In vineyard parlance, this branch is known as a "cane". The nurseryman cuts out a ten to twelve inch segment of such a cane and plants it in either soil or sand for three months, during which time leaves grow above and roots below. It is now spoken of as "rootstock". At this stage of growth it can be removed from its bed and stored in a cool and moist environment for months, to be available to the grower at a planting time of his choosing. To the rootstock will be grafted cuttings of Vitis vinifera, such as Chardonnay or Cabernet Sauvignon, that will determine the variety of grape it will produce.

Photo:Gerardo Ramirez, rootstock sorter

This rootstock is a descendant of native North American vines found by the Pilgrims growing profusely in the New World. However, their grapes were of such poor quality that the growers relied entirely on cuttings brought from Europe in an attempt to produce a satisfactory wine. These imported varietals consistently failed, withering and dying within two or three years. Thomas Jefferson knew this sequence well. In the mid-nineteenth century, native American plants found their way first to Kew Gardens in London and then to the Continent. Presumably, they carried with them the plant-louse phylloxera, an insect that destroys the vine by attacking its roots. These plants acted as carriers for a pest to which they themselves had become resistant.

 The scourge spread through France and almost destroyed their wine industry during the 1860's and 70's. Vineyards in bordering countries also suffered. Some of the infected plants reached California, possibly when the pioneer vintner Agoston Haraszthy brought cuttings from Europe to invigorate the California wine industry. The phylloxera then decimated California vineyards in the 1880's and 90's. All seemed lost until someone, probably American Charles Riley, recognized that the original American plants were the only survivors. When used as rootstock, their grafts of susceptable varieties of grapes were protected. Today, in all areas of the world where phylloxera is present in the soil, rootstock of native American origin has grafted to it the varieties of wine grapes originating abroad.*Photo: Frank Emmolo, Pioneer rootstock Grower*

This rootstock, while dormant, is planted in early spring. The vineyard outlines have already been defined, for stakes have been placed in the ground at four to eight foot intervals in rows six to ten feet apart.

The six-foot intervals between vines has generally been the rule in the California Coastal Valleys. However, recent experience with closer spacing in the French style have found this greater vine density well supported by the rich river-bed soils. The six to ten foot interval between rows allows room for farm machinery to manuever during cultivating, spraying, and picking. Narrower rows require special smaller equipment.

Next, a watering system is installed. There are two basic types. The drip system can be recognized by the black plastic tubing stretching from stake to stake not far above the ground. It has become the workhorse of vineyard irrigation, for it is economical and efficient with its stream of drops falling close to the plants. Where frost is seldom a problem, such as high on hillsides, irrigation by drip alone is sufficient.

Overhead sprinklers use more water than the drip system because water is sprayed over the total vineyard area, rather than only on each plant. Thus, with new plants much of the water is not utilized, but as the vines mature and roots grow laterally, water utilization becomes efficient. However, this irrigation system has a second important function, unique to it - to protect the vines against the damage of frost which can kill developing grape buds and new growth. When the temperature drops to freezing and below, the water constantly falling on the plant freezes on its surfaces, and in so doing, gives up heat to the plant. This heat (heat of fusion) prevents the plant temperature from falling below 32 degrees, critically important in late spring when new shoots are out and the fruit is beginning to form. Paradoxically, when summer heat is excessive, sprinkler water acts as a protective coolant.

Both drip and overhead irrigation are seen in recently planted vineyards where the growers wish to utilize the advantages of each system, although installation is more costly. Then there are those vineyards where the growers find that soil conditions, valley location, and type of grapes are such that the vines seem to flourish without irrigation and depend entirely on ground water, referred to as "dry farming".

However, most vineyards require that water be readily and constantly available, not only to nourish the vines during the heat of summer, but to meet the large and sudden demands of sprinklers in nights of frost danger. Reservoirs dot the floor of the Valleys. In anticipation of summer needs, they are filled during the winter months by well and river water when rain replenishes the rivers and water table.

Planting is now begun. It is late winter or early spring. At each stake, a hole ten to twelve inches in depth is spaded out by the experienced vineyard worker. The dormant rootstock has been taken from the nursery cold storage and its roots are trimmed to fit easily into the hole. Its planting depth is such that two buds are above ground level.

The plant is then covered with a protective mound of soil from which shoots and leaves will emerge as soon as roots take hold. The soil mound protects tender emerging shoots from spring weather extremes, giving roots a chance to grow before leaves reach sunlight.

After three months of spring weather, the rootstock has thoroughly rooted and lush growth of new shoots and leaves flare out from the mounds. The vineyard resembles rows of bouquets. In late July and early August it is time to "bud", or graft, the desired grape variety to the rootstock. We must be reminded that the rootstock has been picked primarily for its ability to resist phylloxera, and it is the graft that will determine the variety of grape to be harvested.

Workers with special "budding" experience return to the vineyard. They carry in their work boxes short cane sections of the desired specific grape variety. Each cane bears five or six buds that are to be the grafts. We have been calling these branches "shoots" during the growing season. However, as grape growth matures, new buds for the next year's growth are formed and lie dormant along the now woody "cane". These canes may be cut from nearby vines or may be brought from a distance, possibly having been in cold storage for the winter.

The plant is cleared of dirt to expose several inches of straight trunk, and a point for budding is picked just above ground level and below the leafy growth. Then, with a deft flick of the wrist, the "budder" slices a bud from his grafting cane, the bud flying into the air, to be caught and usually placed between his lips - all in one rhythmic motion with his cutting hand. The rhythm continues as he cuts a "V" notch into the rootstock with his budding knife.

The bud is then fitted snugly into the rootstock notch, to be held in place by plastic or rubber tape firmly wrapped around it, with the tip of the bud protruding. The bouquet of shoots and leaves is trimmed somewhat, leaving enough green leaf surface to make use of sunlight for photosynthesis. The bud is covered again with a small mound of protective soil.

When the grower decides to change the variety of grape in his vineyard and do this without planting new rootstock, he can "bud over". The technique is called "T budding". First, most of the plant is removed by sectioning the trunk two to three feet above the ground. The remaining trunk is disease-free and its original rootstock has an extensive root system ready to support the new varietal growth to the degree that a bud on each side will "take". "T" cuts are made in the bark and buds are secured in place with tape. New growth aggressively takes off and fruit production is speeded.

The following spring we watch for the appearance of new growth from the grafted bud. When shoots and leaves poke through the soil, the rootstock is cut off above the graft to force the grafted bud growth. The fragile plant must be protected from rodents and extremes of wind and sun. Therefore, either a milk carton or a plastic tube is placed surrounding the plant. This "protector" tends to direct vine growth upward towards the light.

Some growers have found that they can speed up a marketable harvest by one year if the grafting process is done in a nursery, rather than in the field. Thus, the rootstock is planted with the specific graft already in place and growing. This is accomplished by "bench grafting" in the nursery. One method is to notch the rootstock and the cane with its bud in "tongue and groove" fashion and to fit them snugly end to end, then to be sealed in place with hot wax. The budded rootstock is then returned to the nursery growing conditions, requiring great care until transfer to vineyard soil months later.

Mid-summer finds the well-tended growing tip of the vine at the top of the stake. This is often called "first year up the stake". By selective pruning, its vertical growth is cut back to the trellis wire, and lateral shoot growth is encouraged during the plant's second year. Second year pruning will determine the final vine configuration.

By the third year after planting the rootstock, production of fruit sufficient to harvest begins, increasing over the next three years before leveling out. A vine may produce quality wine for many years - even to four decades - its life usually limited by disease, aging processes not unlike the human being, and finally, economics. In the latter case, changes in the public taste may make a particular type of wine no longer saleable.

A visitor in the Coastal Valleys sees row upon row of vines, all very ordered and neat. Yet here the sameness ends, for each grower has his own ideas as to the form his plants should be given by the pruning shears. Pruning takes place when the plants are dormant, sometime between December and March, the time often varying with the availability of workers. As one travels through the vineyards, three styles of pruning are recognized: head trained, spur pruned; head trained, cane pruned; and cordon trained, spur pruned.

The vine is "head trained, spur pruned" when it seems to stand by itself in rows without a wire trellis. It requires only a single stake for support during its early years. All branches (canes) are cut back to form "spurs", each spur having two buds. From these buds the shoots will spring. At full growth, each vine resembles a head with cascading unruly hair.

Such pruning is old style and comes down to us from at least Roman times. Many such plants, gnarled with age and planted in an era before the reliable virus-free and phylloxera resistant rootstocks were easily available, are likely to be replaced with plants trained in another fashion. However, this method is not likely to disappear, for the head-pruned vine carries well the heavy clusters of a grape such as Zinfandel.

A vine is "head trained, cane pruned" when one or more (usually two to four) of the canes from the last year's growth are preserved, shortened and tied to the trellis wires running the length of each row. Each year a different pair of canes is chosen, picked for hardiness and pliability that allows them to be bent and tied to the trellis wire. From these canes will come the shoots that will bear most of the fruit. Four to six spurs are left on the main trunk to produce the canes for the year ahead.

As the cane-pruned plants fill out, the rows of vines are not clearly delineated unless some of the flowing growth is cut back to allow the tractors to move between them for weed control and spraying, and to allow sunshine to reach the developing clusters. Of the three pruning methods, cane pruning requires the most experience and care, yet is still widely used in our Valleys.

The remaining pruning method widely used throughout California is known as "cordon trained, spur pruned". Here, one shoot is trained out on each side of the main trunk along the trellis wire. The trunk above is eliminated and the canes are permanently tied to the wires. By the second year, these "cordons" have a trunk-like appearance and bear all of the fruit on their shoots. Field Marigolds as ground cover add orange to the well established yellows of mustard.

The cordon pruned vine is trained vertically by preserving only the spurs on top of the cordons, usually four or more on each side. At full growth these rows of vines retain their symmetry, making it possible for mechanical picking machines to work efficiently as they shake the grapes from the vines. To the lover of order, the cordon-trained vineyard has the greatest aesthetic appeal.

As the new shoots develop in the spring, a primary concern of the grower is protection against frost, particularly on the floor of the valleys where the coldest air tends to settle. Originally, heaters warmed the valley floors, burning kerosene at first, and more recently, diesel oil. Sometime in the 1950's, motor driven propellers appeared, often World War II airplane engines. These "wind machines" act by mixing the lower cold air with the warm layer above, providing critical degrees of warmth to the vines. Heaters placed on the vineyard periphery aid in providing warmth as the fans distribute their heat. However, maximum frost protection is provided by the overhead "rainbird" watering system, easily the growers' first choice when sufficient water is available.

Powdery mildew is one of the scourges of the vineyard. Its spores are always present and can attack the vine and the fruit during the growing season before the fruit ripens, making it unmarketable. Sulfur, a natural mineral, provides time-honored protection, applied as a powder or as a fine spray from a tractor or crop-duster, and often at night when the air is quiet. A valley vineyard will require such crop protection at least five times a year.

New caves burrow into the hills. Chinese immigrants came to California searching for gold. They next built a railroad. Then they came to the Napa Valley, and with pick and shovel, hollowed out the mountains to create the perfect environment to store wine. Today, this tunneling auger with an expert at the wheel who guides his machine by laser, constantly drills into rock hillsides of the California Valleys. Caves provide a constant 59 degree temperature and an air moisture so high that evaporation is miniscule. The labor-intensive need to "top the barrels" is reduced along with expensive air conditioning.

Photo: Cave Driller Dale Wondergem

Veraison has occurred in the summer warmth, yet we still have morning dew. The grape is maturing. In late July white Chardonnay and red Pinot Noir declare their colors. The other red grapes, such as Cabernet Sauvignon and Zinfandel have a few more weeks to go before they "turn".

It is late August, September, or early October. The grapes must now be picked, for their sugar content has reached critical levels. This measurement is made with a refractometer - a hand-held instrument that allows light to pass through a drop of juice. The molecules of sugar bend (refract) the light on a scale that assigns the sugar concentration. This reading happens to be approximately twice the concentration of alcohol expected in the finished wine.

Photo:Veteran Grower Nathan Fay

The readings are commonly given in "Brix" units, representing percent. As soon as 16 Brix is reached, increasingly careful attention is paid to the refractometer. Depending on the variety of grape, a reading of 19 to 24 calls for timely decisions. Grapes for champagne are picked at about 19 Brix; for table wines at 21 to 24; for "late harvest" dessert wines at 27 and higher. Growers are paid according to optimum sugar and acid concentrations on delivery to the winery.

"The pick" is a strenuous time for growers and workers, particularly when weather variations bring optimum sugar concentrations of the various varietals to a simultaneous peak. And this often happens. Fortunately, the different "microclimates" and many varieties of grapes grown in the Valleys usually allow the harvesting to spread out through late August, September, October, and even early November.   This timetable allows for the most efficient use of vineyard labor. Chardonnay and other whites along with red Pinot Noir ripen first, to be followed by Merlot, Zinfandel, and Cabernet Sauvignon.

Picking begins earliest in the warmer microclimates north of Sonoma and St. Helena and in the Livermore Valley. The Carneros vineyards, cooled by the water of San Pablo Bay and breezes from the Pacific Ocean, tend to ripen slowly and may be among the last to be harvested.

The vineyard workers are very special. The majority live nearby and work year round in the vineyards. There is plenty to do. Temporary workers come in for the harvest. The work is particularly demanding at that time, and payment is in direct proportion to the amount of grapes picked. Often the older more experienced workers are the most productive - fine examples for the stronger young men.

When their pick fills the gondola, it is trucked to the winery with all haste to begin the crush promptly. St. Helena's Main Street, at the height of the crush, is a sight one always remembers - a line of slow-moving trucks with grape-filled gondolas trying to reach a particular winery, with worried drivers concerned about their load's prolonged exposure to the sun.

Photo: Vineyard Foreman Lupe Maldonado

The machine-picker is becoming less of a novelty as it slaps or shakes the grape clusters loose from the vines. Because the grape skins are often broken in the process, speed and cool temperatures are required to prevent the early onset of fermentation by vineyard yeasts. Thus, this is often a night operation and remains unseen by the casual passerby.

The art and science of picking constantly evolves. A few growers are now picking by hand under fluorescent lights through the late night and very early morning. Why? It is cool and less fatiguing. The berries remain cool and firm all the way to the winery where they are promptly processed by a fresh winery crew. There is a physical price, though, for sleep patterns of viticulturists and workers are greatly disturbed.

The grapes must be crushed, pressed, and fermented to become wine.

The term "crush" refers only to the first step in the hands of the winemaker. It is the process of removing the stems, with their bitter tannins, and simultaneously breaking the skins of the grapes, so that for the first time the juice begins to flow. This mix of skins, seeds, pulp and juice is referred to as the "must".

The very small or amateur winemaker uses a hand or small motor driven machine which turns rollers that crush the grapes, dropping them into a perforated hammock where paddles knock off the stems. The grapes drop through the perforations, leaving the stems behind. The stems are returned to the vineyard as a nutritional supplement.

Photo: Home winery workers Mary and Richard Williams

This large auger moves the fresh fruit into the winery crusher and de-stemmer, a rotating cylinder, the wall of which is really a strainer with perforations just large enough to allow the grapes to pass through. High speed spinning paddles inside the cylinder separate grapes and stems. The stems are ejected while the grapes drop through the perforations. Crushing of the grape in the past took place between rollers, but today the grape skins are simply broken by the action of the paddles as the winemaker pursues gentleness in his art.

After crushing, grapes destined to produce a red wine take a course different from that of the white. We must be reminded that with the exception of Alicante Bouschet, the juice of all wine grapes is initially white. Only through contact of the white juice with the broken red skin is red wine created. This occurs during fermentation, and red skins are not removed until the press that follows. Conversely, in the creation of most white wines, skins and juice are promptly separated in the press before fermentation. A few white wines benefit from skin-juice contact, and pressing may be delayed for nine to twelve hours, but no longer. To make a white wine from a red grape, such as White Zinfandel, the red grapes are treated as if they were white, with prompt pressing and skin removal. A Rosē results when fermentation of the red grape is allowed to go on 24 hours or more. Pressing and skin removal take place in the middle of the fermentation process.

```
WHITE GRAPE------------------CRUSH---------------PRESS------------------FERMENT
RED GRAPE--------------------CRUSH----------------FERMENT-------------PRESS
```

"Pressing" refers to the process of squeezing the grapes for their juice, leaving behind skins, pulp and seeds. The small family winery will probably still use the time-honored hand-driven basket press. It requires elbow grease. The juice that flows from the press as soon as the grapes are poured in and before direct pressure is applied is known as the "free run". This juice is considered to be of special quality. It may be further processed separately or returned to the main run.

Photo: Family winery worker-author Dick Lyon.

After the juice has passed through the strainers to remove any seeds or skins that have slipped through the press, it is transferred to a stainless steel holding tank. Compressed seeds and skins left in the press make up the "cake', also known as "pomace" to be lifted out of the press and then usually returned to the vineyard as fertilizer.

The commercial winery has large power-driven presses. The press in greatest use is simply a closed cylinder that rotates to increase the mix. A bladder inflates inside. It compresses the grapes against the cylinder walls. The expressed juice is then pumped into holding tanks.

A critical process in the creation of wine is "fermentation" - the conversion of sugars (glucose and fructose) to alcohol and the gas CO_2. An important by-product of this reaction is heat, demanding the constant attention of the winemaker. We expect the alcohol in all table wines to ultimately reach a concentration of 11 to 14%. The rate of fermentation is monitored by measuring the decreasing sugar concentrations with the time-honored hydrometer. In the winery it becomes a "saccharometer".

The agents of this process are usually special yeasts, carefully propagated and prepared so that their action can be directed and predicted. It was not long ago that winemakers relied entirely on the naturally occurring yeasts that appear on the grapes as they ripen. Today, the experience with natural vineyard yeasts has increased. The winemaker has the privilege of choice between the dependable commercial yeast and a natural yeast that has made its home in his vineyard.

Photo: Judge Thomas Kongsgaard

White juice is promptly readied for fermentation. Thirty-six hours is often allowed for settling and removal of sediment before the juice is pumped into stainless steel tanks or small barrels. The family winery, after allowing overnight settling to take place in their single vat, will often transfer the juice to oak barrels for the fermentation process. In both cases, if yeast is to be added, this is done promptly, and fermentation begins.

Because skins, pulp and seeds have been removed in the pressing process, turbulence of white fermentation is mild compared to that of the reds. CO_2 escapes through valves (fermentation locks) in the steel containers or through a glass ball-valve kept in the "bung hole" of each barrel. Unlike the red fermentation, heat production is not a great problem. Tank temperatures of 45 to 65 degrees F are not difficult to maintain. Temperature-control jackets on steel tanks allow the cellarmaster to regulate the rate of fermentation - the cooler, the slower. With temperatures kept in the upper 50 degree range, fermentation may be stretched from days to weeks. In the family winery, temperature control is limited to keeping the winery itself cool.

Red fermentation is a very active process, for skins, pulp and seeds have not yet been removed by pressing and these still interact with the juice. Thus, the bubbling surface of the fermenting liquid is purposely kept well below the top of the tank so that overflow does not occur during the peak of activity.

Unique to red fermentation is the firm "cap" of skins and seeds that bubble up and concentrate on the surface. This cap requires constant attention at the height of fermentation. The small winemaker breaks up the cap manually with a plunger at least two to four times a day by "punching down". This stirs the mix at the same time as it encourages CO_2 to escape. The large winery accomplishes this with a stream of juice directed from above as it is pumped from the bottom of the same tank. This is called "pumping over"

Photo: Carol Lyon, puncher-downer.

Heat, too, is a major problem in the early stages of red fermentation, for if allowed to "run away", temperatures could reach above 100 degrees F and destroy both yeast and wine. The small winemaker keeps his winery at 50 to 60 degrees F, and with a small tank, adequate cooling is usually achieved. On the other hand, in the large winery, metal cooling jackets surround the tanks for constant and accurate temperature control, usually in the 75 to 85 degree range.

In five to seven days, the red fermentation process slows itself as sugar levels reach close to zero. The winemaker may decide to press promptly or to leave the skins and juice in place, usually to give a deeper color to the final wine. This may take one to four weeks. After pressing, the juice is usually transferred to oak barrels for completion of fermentation and the beginning of the aging process.

As fermentation comes to an end, requiring three to fourteen days for the reds and ten days to six weeks for the whites, the attention of the winemaker is directed toward clarifying the wine. Clarification is often begun by "racking". This is the process of allowing the wine "to settle", and then transferring the cleared wine to a second barrel or tank. This procedure is repeated at intervals with further clearing with each transfer. The sediment left behind, much of it burned-out yeast, is known as "the lees".

Unwanted air is eliminated as much as possible by periodic "topping"- adding small amounts of wine of similar variety and vintage, thus keeping the barrel full. At the same time, the short exposure of the wine to air during the racking and pumping procedure is considered to be beneficial.

Photo: Winemaker Dean Sylvester

To speed the clearing process, clarifiers may be added to the wine. For white wines, a clay known as Bentonite is most often used as an absorber, pulling with it to the bottom of tank or barrel the undesired elements. The wine is then racked off, leaving Bentonite and its captives on the bottom.

For further clarification, filtration through diotomaceous earth (as in filtration of the usual swimming pool water) is perhaps the most used process. Next comes filtration through special pads that act functionally as a combination of filter and blotter. The centrifuge, most costly and efficient, is also used in some of the largest wineries. Its high speed rotations and resulting centrifugal force quickly and continuously separate out suspended matter. "Fining" refers to the finishing step in clarification of fine wine--the use of such agents as casein or isinglass for whites; gelatin and egg whites for reds.

Most white wines are bottled between three and twelve months after harvest. Bottling of red wine is rarely done within the year. Each winemaker has his or her style, the sum total of numerous decisions - whether to age in stainless steel or oak? Should we use an old or a new barrel? Should it be American or French oak? Should we use a large oak barrel with relatively small wood surface with respect to volume, or should it be a small barrel with its maximum "woody" effect on the final wine? And how long should we leave the wine in any one or a sequence of these containers? The large winery relies on experienced "tasters" and an array of chemical tests for acidity, pH, alcohol content and sugar concentration. The very small vintner relies on his eye for clarity and color, nose for aroma, and mouth for taste.

Photos: Immortal Winemaker-Teacher Andre Tchelistcheff tasting with student Winemaker Marco Capelli.

A second fermentation process may start by itself during the months in the barrel after primary fermentation has ended. This process is referred to as "malo-lactic" fermentation. The agent of this phase of fermentation, the lactobacillus, may come from the vineyard into the winery on skins, or be simply at home on winery equipment. When the winemaker wishes to keep full control and not depend on the probable introduction of lactobacillus, he will add the cultured organism with or soon after the primary fermentation, and follow the secondary fermentation process carefully. His intent? To convert a "fruity" malic acid to a softer "velvety" lactic acid. This is a phase of winemaking where one finds great differences of opinion among the winemakers as to the need, the timing, and the eventual control of the process.

Photo: Veteran Grower Angelo Regusci

To create champagne, we must first create a wine from grapes such as Pinot Noir, Chardonnay, and Pinot Blanc. From the start, there is a bit of the grand touch to which these stately tanks attest. Because yeast and sugar are added to make possible a second fermentation, these grapes are the earliest picked at Brix close to 19 in order that the acidity remain high and alcohol low.

In the champagne cave, "riddling" during the day almost never stops. In each eight hours Ramon Viera rotates 30,000 bottles 45 degrees as he gradually brings each bottle to the vertical, neck down. Thus, the sediment from the secondary fermentation is undisturbed as it settles into the bottle neck. There it is frozen in cold brine. The cap is removed and the sediment is "disgorged" as CO_2 pressure in the bottle pops it out. The final cork is then placed.

Most wines carry the imprint of their days, months, and at times, years in the barrel. These barrels are usually of white oak and are imported from France. However, "coopers" (barrel makers) are now developing this trade in the wine valleys of the west. American oak is now a worthy competitor, especially since the practice of air-seasoning for two years has replaced the rapid "kiln-drying" method used in the spirits industry. The oak is first cut to barrel-stave shape. Then, over a wood fire, heat, and water sparingly applied to the wood surfaces, allow the cooper to bend the staves into barrel form, to then be bound tightly in place. The fire can further be used to "toast", not char, the inner barrel surface to the extent that the winemaker desires. Thus, the wood itself and the toasting both leave their marks on the final product.

Bottling is a tedious process. The new bottles arrive in boxes, neck down. They are sterile, for they have been boxed while still cooling after being poured into final form. Inert nitrogen may be used to flush the bottles and thus minimize exposure of wine to air as the bottle is being filled. Bottling is still done by hand in the small family winery with equipment that allows for constant filling of the bottle to a level that leaves space (ullage) for cork placement with a minimum of accompanying air. The commercial winery does this mechanically in a bottling line.

Photo: Home winemaker Judge Thomas Kongsgaard and Winemaker son John

The corks are driven in by machine or by hand, and the tinned seal is fixed in place with an electrically driven helper. Labeling is accomplished either by hand or machine. Bottles go into the case, bottoms up in order to keep the corks wet and thus produce a tight seal against air.

Labels contain important information regulated by federal law in close cooperation with the wine industry. Each wine must have a brand name. If the variety of grape is given, such as Chardonnay or Zinfandel, the wine must contain a minimum of 75% of that particular grape. The wine then may be spoken of as a "varietal". "Appellation of origin" refers to the specific viticultural area. If the viticultural area is designated as a county, then 75% of the grapes must be grown and processed in that county. This requirement increases to 85% if the appellation given is that of an "established viticultural area". These areas are not limited by county boundaries. Napa Valley, Carneros, and Livermore Valley are examples of such "areas". When the "California" appellation is given, 100% of the wine must be made from grapes grown and processed within the state. Finally, the name of the bottler and address of the bottling location must be given. Alcoholic content designation is the rule.

If the vintage year is given, 95% of the wine must be of that year's growth. "Estate Bottled" requires that all of the grapes be grown in the same viticultural area and in vineyards owned or controlled by the winery that completely processes the wine from crush to bottle. "Private Reserve" has no legal requirement, but is often used to designate what the winery considers to be a special bottling. Finally, such terms as "bottled by", "made by", etc., are unrestrictive when compared to "produced and bottled by" which requires that the bottler has fermented and finished 75% of the wine on the premises.

"Wine of California....
      inimitable fragrance and soft fire
      ....and the wine is
      bottled poetry"
                    —Robert Louis Stevenson

Months, years or decades may pass before the cork is pulled and the winemaker's success in channeling the grower's skill with the vagaries of sun, rain, and soil becomes apparent. Certainly, a good part of our fascination with wine is in knowing that no amount of study and skill can remove the roll of chance and serendipity from a process which remains as much alchemy as science. Our best wines, like our best moments, are not to be understood but rather to be deeply enjoyed.

GLOSSARY

Appellation. Geographic areas, usually counties, designated by law, defining where a particular grape is grown. In order that "appellation" be given on the label, 85% of the grapes must be grown in that area.

Bud. The embryonic site on the grapevine from which the shoot will take its origin.

Bung Hole. The opening in the top of the barrel through which it is filled and emptied. Its stopper is known as the bung.

Cake. Pomace in cake-like form at completion of the press.

Cane. Originally a shoot, now dormant with a woody consistency at the time the fruit fully ripens.

Cap. The dense layer of skins, pulp, and seeds that forms on the surface of fermenting red juice.

Cooper. Barrel maker.

Crushing. The breaking of the grape skins between rollers, and coincident separtion of stems to be discarded.

Cutting. A section of a cane with buds suitable for grafting.

Enology. The science and practice of making wine.

Fining. The process of improving the wine clarity with agents such as egg white, gelatin, isinglass, and casein.

Free-run. The juice that first flows from the press as it is filled and before any pressure is applied.

Grower. The master of the vineyards, from rootstock to picking.

Lees: Sediment collecting in the bottom of a barrel or tank. A wine is said to be "on the lees" if the sediment is left in place and not removed as with racking.

Must. The juice of the red grape with skins. pulp, and seeds after crushing and ready to be fermented; the crushed white grapes and, after pressing, the white juice ready for fermentation.

Pressing. The squeezing of the grapes by pressure, freeing the juice and leaving skins and seeds behind.

Phylloxera. The plant-louse that decimated vineyards here and abroad in the later half of the last century, and again here in California in recent years.

Pomace. The residue of skin and seeds after pressing.

Pruning. The removal of unwanted old growth during the dormant season, which adjusts crop loads and shapes and directs the growth of the vine.

Pump over. This occurs during red fermentation, the juice being pumped from the bottom of the tank and then under pressure sprayed over the cap.

Punching down. Physically breaking up the cap on the surface of the fermenting red must.

Racking. In the process of clearing the wine, the juice is transferred from barrel to barrel, leaving the sediment, or lees, behind.

Shoot. New growth from the pruned plant, from which leaves first appear, followed by clusters of grapes, usually two to each shoot.

Spur. When canes are trimmed during pruning, their bases are left, usually with two buds. These buds then produce the next year's growth as shoots.

Topping. The process of adding like wine to the barrel to compensate for evaporation, thus minimizing the possibility of air harming the aging process.

Ullage. The small air space allowed between wine and cork in the bottle.

Vintage. The year the wine was produced. The "vintage year" may be given on the label if 95% of the wine was of that year. 5% is allowed for the additions with topping.

Viticulture. The study and science of vine growth.

Vitis. Genus of woody vines, including the grapevine.

    labrusca--the "foxy" native American variety.

    vnifera--the varieties of European origin suitable for table wines.

Winemaster. The designer and director of the the finished wine, beginning to end.